READ & RESPOND

T0322925

Helping children discover the pleasure and power of reading

ZANIB MIAN

ILLUSTRATED BY
NASAYA MAFARIDIK

PLANET OMAR

ACCIDENTAL TROUBLE MAGNET

FOR AGES 7–9

Published in the UK by Scholastic Education, 2023

Scholastic Distribution Centre, Bosworth Avenue, Tournament Fields, Warwick, CV34 6UQ

Scholastic Ireland, 89E Lagan Road, Dublin Industrial Estate, Glasnevin, Dublin, D11 HP5F

SCHOLASTIC and associated logos are trademarks and/or registered trademarks of Scholastic Inc.

© 2023 Scholastic

www.scholastic.co.uk

1 2 3 4 5 6 7 8 9   3 4 5 6 7 8 9 0 1 2

Printed and bound by Ashford Colour Press
This book is made of materials from well-managed,
FSC®-certified forests and other controlled sources.

A CIP catalogue record for this book is available from the British Library.
ISBN 978-0702-32066-8

Extracts from *The National Curriculum in England, English Programme of Study* © Crown Copyright. Reproduced under the terms of the Open Government Licence (OGL). http://www.nationalarchives.gov.uk/doc/open-government-licence/version/3

Due to the nature of the web, we cannot guarantee the content or links of any site mentioned. We strongly recommend that teachers check websites before using them in the classroom.

Authors Sally Burt and Debbie Ridgard
Editorial team Rachel Morgan, Vicki Yates, Audrey Stokes, Sarah Snashall and Julia Roberts
Series designer Andrea Lewis
Typesetter QBS Learning
Illustrator Clive Goodyer

Acknowledgements
The publishers gratefully acknowledge permission to reproduce the following material:
Reproduced with permission of **Hachette Childrens Group** through PLSclear for the use of the text extracts, illustrations and cover from *Planet Omar Accidental Trouble Magnet* Text copyright © Zanib Mian, 2019; Illustrations copyright © Nasaya Mafaridik, 2019
Every effort has been made to trace copyright holders for the works reproduced in this book, and the publishers apologise for any inadvertent omissions.

For supporting online resources go to:
www.scholastic.co.uk/read-and-respond/books/planet-omar/online-resources
Access key: Locate

CONTENTS ▼

How to use Read & Respond in your classroom...

Read & Respond provides teaching ideas related to a specific well-loved children's book. Each Read & Respond book is divided into the following sections:

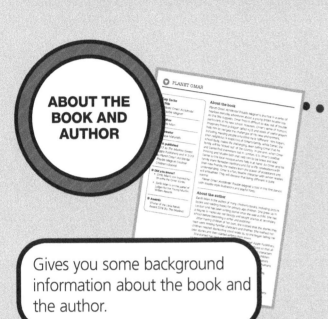

ABOUT THE BOOK AND AUTHOR

Gives you some background information about the book and the author.

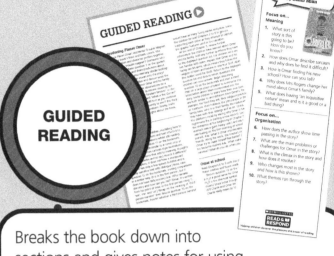

GUIDED READING

Breaks the book down into sections and gives notes for using it, ideal for use with the whole class. A bookmark has been provided on page 12 containing **comprehension** questions. The children can be directed to refer to these as they read. Find comprehensive guided reading sessions on the supporting online resources.

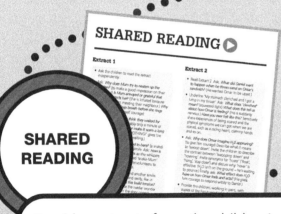

SHARED READING

Provides extracts from the children's book with associated notes for focused work. There is also one non-fiction extract that relates to the children's book.

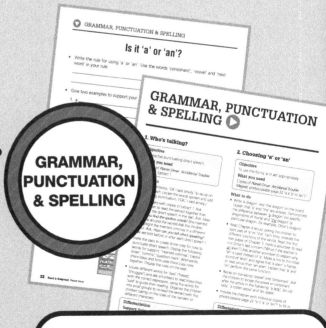

GRAMMAR, PUNCTUATION & SPELLING

Provides word-level work related to the children's book so you can teach grammar, punctuation, spelling and **vocabulary** in context.

PLOT, CHARACTER & SETTING

Contains activity ideas focused on the plot, characters and the setting of the story.

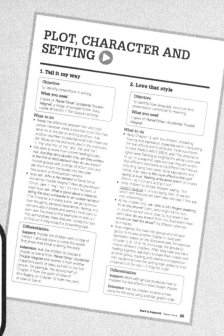

TALK ABOUT IT

Oracy, **fluency**, and speaking and listening activities. These activities may be based directly on the children's book or be broadly based on the themes and concepts of the story.

GET WRITING

Provides writing activities related to the children's book. These activities may be based directly on the children's book or be broadly based on the themes and concepts of the story.

ASSESSMENT

Contains short activities that will help you assess whether the children have understood concepts and curriculum objectives. They are designed to be informal activities to feed into your planning.

SUPPORTING ONLINE RESOURCE

Online you can find a host of supporting documents including planning information, comprehensive guided reading sessions and guidance on teaching reading.

www.scholastic.co.uk/read-and-respond/books/planet-omar/online-resources
Access key: Locate

Help children develop a love of reading for pleasure.

Activities

The activities follow the same format:

- **Objective:** the objective for the lesson. It will be based upon a curriculum objective, but will often be more specific to the focus being covered.

- **What you need:** a list of resources you need to teach the lesson, including photocopiable pages.

- **What to do:** the activity notes.

- **Differentiation:** this is provided where specific and useful differentiation advice can be given to support and/or extend the learning in the activity. Differentiation by providing additional adult support has not been included as this will be at a teacher's discretion based upon specific children's needs and ability, as well as the availability of support.

The activities are numbered for reference within each section and should move through the text sequentially – so you can use the lesson while you are reading the book. Once you have read the book, most of the activities can be used in any order you wish.

CURRICULUM LINKS

Section	Activity	Curriculum objectives
Guided reading		Comprehension: To develop positive attitudes to reading and understanding of what they read.
Shared reading	1	Comprehension: To discuss words and phrases that capture the reader's interest and imagination.
	2	Comprehension: To identify how language, structure and presentation contribute to meaning.
	3	Comprehension: To identify how language, structure and presentation contribute to meaning.
	4	Comprehension: To retrieve and record information from non-fiction.
Grammar, punctuation & spelling	1	Vocabulary, grammar and punctuation: To introduce inverted commas to punctuate direct speech.
	2	Vocabulary, grammar and punctuation: To use the forms *a* or *an* according to whether the next word begins with a consonant or a vowel.
	3	Vocabulary, grammar and punctuation: To explore word families, showing how they are related in form or meaning.
	4	Vocabulary, grammar and punctuation: To express time using conjunctions, adverbs or prepositions.
	5	Comprehension: To check that the text makes sense to them, discussing their understanding and explaining the meaning of words in context.
	6	Spelling: To add the suffix ly to an adjective to form an adverb, using known spelling rules.
Plot, character & setting	1	Comprehension: To identify conventions in writing.
	2	Comprehension: To identify how language, structure and presentation contribute to meaning.
	3	Comprehension: To draw inferences such as inferring characters' feelings, thoughts and motives from their actions, and justifying inferences with evidence.
	4	Comprehension: To identify conventions in a wide range of books.
	5	Comprehension: To identify conventions in a wide range of books.
	6	Comprehension: To draw inferences such as inferring characters' feelings, thoughts and motives from their actions, and justifying inferences with evidence.
	7	Comprehension: To identify themes in a wide range of books.
	8	Comprehension: To draw inferences such as inferring characters' feelings, thoughts and motives from their actions, and justifying inferences with evidence.

Section	Activity	Curriculum objectives
Talk about it	1	Spoken language: To ask relevant questions to extend their understanding and knowledge.
	2	Spoken language: To maintain attention and participate actively in collaborative conversations.
	3	Spoken language: To use spoken language to develop understanding through speculating, hypothesising, imagining, and exploring ideas.
	4	Spoken language: To maintain attention and participate actively in collaborative conversations.
	5	Spoken language: To participate in discussions and role play.
	6	Spoken language: To give well-structured explanations.
Get writing	1	Composition: To discuss writing similar to that which they are planning.
	2	Composition: To use simple organisational devices.
	3	Composition: To discuss and record ideas.
	4	Composition: To read aloud their own writing.
	5	Composition: To proofread for errors.
	6	Composition: To assess the effectiveness of their own and others' writing suggesting improvements.
Assessment	1	Spoken language: To speak audibly and fluently.
	2	Composition: To evaluate and edit by proposing changes to grammar and vocabulary to improve consistency, including the accurate use of pronouns in sentences.
	3	Comprehension: To use dictionaries to check the meaning of words that they have read.
	4	Composition: To write narratives, creating settings, characters and plot.
	5	Spoken language: To use spoken language to develop understanding.
	6	Comprehension: To understand what they read.

Key facts

● **Title**
Planet Omar: Accidental Trouble Magnet

● **Author**
Zanib Mian

● **Illustrator**
Nasaya Mafaridik

● **First published**
2017 as *The Muslims* (Sweet Apple Publishers) and in 2019 as *Planet Omar: Accidental Trouble Magnet* (Hodder Children's Books)

● **Did you know?**
- Zanib Mian's son inspired her to write the Omar stories.
- Zanib Mian is on the panel of judges for the Young Muslim Writers Awards.

● **Awards**
Winner of the Little Rebels Award 2018 (As *The Muslims*)

About the book

Planet Omar: Accidental Trouble Magnet is the first in a series of hilarious everyday adventures about a young British Muslim boy. As the title suggests, Omar finds it difficult to stay out of trouble particularly at his new school. However, Omar's sense of humour, imaginary friend (a dragon called H_2O) and stock of useful prayers help him to navigate the challenges of his new environment, including meeting people who think he is 'different'. Mrs Rogers, their neighbour, is suspicious of Omar's family, while Daniel, the school bully, makes life challenging, even telling Omar that his family will be 'kicked out' of the country. In the end, when Omar and Daniel find themselves lost in London, it is Omar's positive thinking and Muslim faith that help him to be brave and lead Daniel to the local mosque where help is at hand. As Omar and his family share Ramadan traditions and Eid ul-Fitr celebrations with their new friends, the readers learn the power of acceptance and understanding. Omar is a fun, lovable character with whom readers will empathise. They will discover that being different is quite normal.

Planet Omar: Accidental Trouble Magnet is told in the first person with doodle-style illustrations and playful fonts.

About the author

Zanib Mian is the author of many children's books, including picture books and reading books for primary age children. She grew up in London and has been writing stories since she was a child. She has a degree in molecular cell biology and taught science at secondary school before becoming a writer and publisher.

After having children of her own, she noticed that the stories they read were missing familiar characters and themes. She realised her children needed stories they could relate to, so she began telling her own stories and then started writing them down.

She started her own publishing company, Sweet Apple Publishers, to promote stories with characters from different cultures so that all children could feel represented. Her stories use colourful characters and humour to explore diversity. She said, 'I write so that children can feel represented in the world they live in, and so that readers can pick up a book that is a window into the lives of fellow humans from different cultures.' Some of her stories have featured on the BBC's CBeebies *Bedtime Stories* show. She lives in Wembley, London, with her family.

About the illustrator

Nasaya Mafaridik loves doodling, witty stories and bright stationery. Her cartoon-style illustrations perfectly complement the hilarious text of the *Planet Omar* stories. She is based in Indonesia.

GUIDED READING ▶

Introducing *Planet Omar*

Introduce *Planet Omar: Accidental Trouble Magnet*. Explore the book's front and back covers, title page, dedication and character profiles together. Ask: *What is a 'trouble magnet'?* (someone who attracts trouble) Raise question 1 on the guided reading bookmark and share predictions about the story. Ask: *Have you read any similar-looking books with illustrations woven into the story?* Read the character profiles and discuss what the children have learned about Omar and his family from them, capturing their observations on a mind map. Create a list of questions raised by the profiles, such as 'What are fondant fancies?' or (for children unfamiliar with Islam) 'What is the Qur'an?' Display the questions and add to it as you continue reading. Revisit the list frequently to see if the story has answered any of the questions. Finally, invite children to share initial thoughts about the book, giving reasons.

Omar at home

Read Chapter 1 to the children, modelling how to incorporate the illustrations and text effects into your expression and delivery whilst still reading fluently. Discuss question 11 on the bookmark. Ask: *How is this style similar to a comic strip or graphic novel?* (It has cartoon-style illustrations, sound effects, fonts that add to meaning, thoughts depicted as asides and so on.) *How is it different?* (It has chapters, it does not have a storyboard layout, it has only a few speech bubbles and is mainly narrative text with dialogue.) Now, raise question 12 on the bookmark, inviting comparisons in a similar way. (It is in the first person, but it does not have daily entries.) Ask: *Who narrates the story and how can you tell?* (Omar: it's written from his point of view, in the first person using 'I', 'we', 'me' and 'us'.) Recap on the meaning of 'third-person narrator' then discuss question 15 on the bookmark. Ponder whether a third-person narrator

would have as many funny asides and jokes. Invite the children to read Chapters 2 to 5 in groups, supporting each other as they attempt to capture the graphic features used in the narrative.

At the end of Chapter 5, review further information the children have learned about Omar and his family. Add any further questions they have to the displayed question list. For children who are not familiar with Islam, explain that Omar and his family are Muslims, which means they follow the religion of Islam and believe in one true God, Allah (the Arabic word for God). Return to the displayed question list and discuss which questions the children can now answer. Begin discussing question 16 on the bookmark and start a mind map on a large piece of paper to summarise the information about Islam incorporated into the story. Invite children to share how their own lives are both similar to and different from Omar's, for example, the food they eat, their religious practices or traditions, their hobbies, the jobs people in their family have, who is in their family, the relationship they have with their siblings and so on. Check the children's recall by asking why Omar is having nightmares (he is starting a new school). Locate the metaphor at the beginning of Chapter 5 ('my stomach was a giant heavy rock') and ask how Omar was feeling on the first morning of school (he was scared). Ask: *What is Omar worried about?* (making friends, doing the work, the teacher) *How does Omar try to make himself feel better?* (by wearing his favourite clothes) Ask: *What makes you feel nervous? What do you do when you are nervous?*

Omar at school

Read Chapters 6 to 9 with the children taking turns. Praise creative and fluent reading.

Discuss question 13 on the bookmark. Ask: *Why is H_2O a good name for Omar's imaginary dragon?* (H_2O is the chemical symbol for water and therefore steam.) Share initial thoughts about Charlie. Ask: *Will Charlie and Omar be friends? Why? What does Charlie really mean by 'OK'?*

Find Omar's description of sarcasm in Chapter 7. Discuss the meaning of 'sarcasm' and ask a volunteer to model how Daniel says 'nice' in a sarcastic manner. Invite children to share how they feel when someone is sarcastic. Ask the children, in pairs, to reflect on question 2 on the bookmark. Share thoughts on what this tells us about Omar and his family. (They don't use sarcasm very often.) Next, ask children with younger siblings to share their experiences and compare them to Omar's relationship with his little brother, Esa. Ask: *What does Mum often do when she's hurrying?* (She says things the wrong way round.) Invite the children to invent silly sentences transposing a verb and noun in a similar way. Ask: *Why does Mum want to take chocolates to their neighbour?* (to introduce themselves) *How does their neighbour respond?* (She is unfriendly.) Discuss why Mrs Rogers might be so unfriendly to her new neighbours.

In Chapter 8, Mum asks Omar if he has done his 'duas' (a form of Muslim prayer). Ask: *Why is Omar being careful about doing his duas at the moment?* (for protection against Daniel) Refer to question 3 on the bookmark and share ideas backed up by evidence from the story. Ask: *Do you think Mum suspects not everything is good at school?* (yes) *Why?* (She makes Omar's favourite food.) Discuss Mrs Rogers' reaction to the biryani. Ask: *Why is she reluctant to taste it?* (fear of something new or different) Encourage the children to discuss how they feel about new or different food. Ask: *What else upsets Mrs Rogers?* (the noise of the children playing football) *Was it a reasonable thing to be upset about?* (Probably not: it may have been loud but wasn't for long.)

Prejudice

Ask the children to read Chapters 10 to 12 independently then ask them to discuss the following questions in groups. *What gives Omar the courage to respond to Daniel throwing sand on his sandwich?* (H_2O) *What was funny about his response?* (It was a clever play on words.) Discuss question 17 on the bookmark. Encourage the children to point out other examples of humour and wordplay as you read on. Ask: *How does Daniel react to Omar's response?* (First, he knocks over Sarah when trying to go for Omar; later he

is rude about Muslims.) *What two things does he say to upset Omar?* (Omar's mum looks like a witch; Muslims will be 'kicked out' of the country.) Introduce the terms 'prejudice' and 'stereotypes'. Sensitively discuss why Daniel is prejudiced against Muslims. (He does not know anything about Muslims; he's heard people being prejudiced against Muslims.) Discuss these issues sensitively in case children have experienced prejudice based on religion, appearance, race or gender. Emphasise that in most cases, people build up prejudices based on stereotypes when they don't take the time to properly understand the situation or people they are talking about. Ask: *How do we know that Charlie is not prejudiced against Muslims?* (from his behaviour towards Omar)

Now ask the children to think about Omar and his family in the car on the way to Manchester. Ask volunteers to talk about similar car journeys they've had with their family. Speculate on whether Daniel would see Omar and his family as very 'different' if he saw them together. Discuss how Daniel might feel hearing Omar and his cousin describing Pakistan. Would he be surprised that it is an alien country to them?

Crisis

Read Chapters 13 to 16 with the children, encouraging the children to take turns reading fluently and expressively.

Discuss what happened to Mrs Rogers and why Omar's parents went to help her when she had been so unfriendly to them. Ask: *Would Mrs Rogers have done the same for Omar's family?* Refer to question 4 on the bookmark and note her changing attitude as she gets to know the family. Return to question 16 on the bookmark, ask: *Is finding out more about something a good way to overcome prejudice?* Then turn to question 5 on the bookmark, inviting examples when it could be both good and bad. Discuss the author's technique of using Charlie's inquisitive nature to teach non-Muslim readers about Ramadan. Ask: *Is reading a story like this a good way to learn factual things about our world?* (Yes, as long as it's well researched; some readers will find this way of learning facts in context more interesting; it can be a good way to discuss the emotions inspired by a subject.) *How is it different to reading a non-fiction book on the subject?* (There is less information, but it can be more personal.) If the children did not know about Ramadan before reading the book, ask them to explain what they have learned. Ask: *What clues tell the reader that Maryam finds fasting difficult?* (She is not doing well at school and loses her temper too easily.) *How does Omar manage his fasting at the weekend?* (not well) *How did Omar's dad react?* (He was supportive and told Omar that Allah would be happy that he'd even tried.)

Moving on

Ask the children to read Chapter 17 in groups. Ask them to try different techniques to capture the textual features. Perhaps different children could take on the direct speech, or read the illustrated words for effect. Raise question 6 on the bookmark. Share answers, for example, explicit references, such as 'seven weeks', the referencing of 'one Wednesday afternoon' (meaning there have been many Wednesdays) and understanding that enough time has passed for everyone to have settled into the Ramadan routine. Then reflect on question 7. Encourage thoughtful responses, (beyond just 'Daniel') that explain what is on Omar's mind.

Read the first four pages of Chapter 18 to the children and ask them to predict how Omar might be a 'trouble magnet' on the trip to the Science Museum. Read to the end of the chapter and ask: *What did happen? Was it Omar's fault? How did Daniel react?* Discuss whether Daniel's reaction is what they expected of 'a bully'. Ask: *What does this suggest about Daniel?* (Daniel is mean because he is unhappy.)

Ask the children to read Chapters 19 to 21 independently. Invite a volunteer to recount the sequence of events. Ask: *How did Omar get them out of trouble?* (First, he tries to remember the way, then he finds a mosque where he knows people will help them.) Invite the children to share how they might react in a similar situation. Talk about

what they could do, emphasising the importance of only talking to people they know or can trust, for example: the police, an official in a museum, underground or similar, or someone in a safe place like a school or place of worship. Ask: *What does Omar learn about Daniel while they are lost?* (He feels neglected because his little sister is unwell.) *Does this justify his behaviour?* (no, but it may explain it) Discuss how talking to people can help us to understand why someone behaves as they do.

Resolution

Read to the end of the story, inviting children to take turns reading. Now reflect on the story as a whole, referring to questions 8 and 9 on the bookmark. Then ask: *Which different elements of the plot are resolved by the end of the story?* Indicate the different threads to consider, such as: Daniel and how he changes, Omar's concern about being 'kicked out' of the country, Omar's need for H_2O, Ramadan, the Eid feast and how it brings everyone together.

Follow this up by reviewing question 10 on the bookmark. Organise the children in groups to discuss different themes, such as prejudice, respect, faith and hope, family, friendship, imagination, being different and so on. Share their ideas and invite suggestions for any other themes they noticed.

Discuss what the children enjoyed about this book using question 14 to help them recap on the story. Reflect with them on anything they learned about Islam if they were not familiar with its traditions before, the characters, the quirky, illustrated writing style, the humour and the wordplay. Return to the list of questions created during reading and discuss the meaning of each word. Consider question 18 on the bookmark and what lessons they have learned. Finally, point out that the last page indicates the book has a sequel. Invite the children to predict Omar's next adventure and survey whether they would enjoy reading it and why.

Planet Omar: Accidental Trouble Magnet

by Zanib Mian

Focus on...
Meaning

1. What sort of story is this going to be? How do you know?

2. How does Omar describe sarcasm and why does he find it difficult?

3. How is Omar finding his new school? How can you tell?

4. Why does Mrs Rogers change her mind about Omar's family?

5. What does having 'an inquisitive nature' mean and is it a good or a bad thing?

Focus on...
Organisation

6. How does the author show time passing in the story?

7. What are the main problems or challenges for Omar in the story?

8. What is the climax in the story and how does it resolve?

9. Who changes most in the story and how is this shown?

10. What themes run through the story?

Planet Omar: Accidental Trouble Magnet

by Zanib Mian

Focus on...
Language and features

11. How do the pictures and text effects help you to enjoy the story?

12. How is the story similar to or different from a diary?

13. Who is Omar's imaginary friend and why does he need him?

14. How does the cover reflect what happens in the story?

Focus on...
Purposes, viewpoints and effects

15. How would the story be different if it had a third-person narrator?

16. How does the author use Omar and his family to teach people about being a Muslim?

17. How does the author use humour and wordplay in the story?

18. Do you think the story has a message for children?

SHARED READING ▶

Extract 1

- Ask the children to read the extract independently.

- Ask: *Why does Mum try to neaten up the children?* (to make a good impression on their neighbour) *Is Mum annoyed or grateful that Maryam corrects her?* (She is irritated because she is focused on meeting their neighbour.) *Why does she take a deep breath before she rings the bell?* (to give herself courage)

- Ask: *How long do you think they waited for the door to open?* (probably only a minute or two) *How does the author make it seem like a long time?* (The repetition of 'NOTHING!' gives the impression of waiting and waiting.)

- Ask: *What is Mum compared to here?* (a snake) Recap on the structure of a simile. Ask: *How is Mum like a snake?* (She hisses as she whispers angrily.) Note she is then called 'snake-Mum' to continue the imagery. Invite volunteers to demonstrate how she speaks.

- Challenge the children to find another simile. ('the door opened quietly and eerily, like in horror movies') *How does this build tension?* ('quietly' and 'eerily' make the reader wonder what they will see when the door opens) *How do you think they felt when they saw Mrs Rogers?* (perhaps a bit of an anti-climax – she is just a little old lady) *How does her response rebuild the tension?* (Her silence is rude and no one knows how to react.)

- Ask the children to re-read the extract aloud in small groups using expression, gestures and body language to support the text.

Extract 2

- Read Extract 2. Ask: *What did Daniel want to happen when he threw sand on Omar's sandwich?* (He wanted Omar to be upset.)

- Underline 'My stomach clenched and I got a lump in my throat'. Ask: *What does 'clenched' mean?* (squeezed tight) *What does this tell us about how Omar is feeling?* (He is suddenly nervous.) *Have you ever felt like this?* Sensitively share experiences of being scared and the physical symptoms we can get when we are scared, such as a racing heart, clammy hands and so on.

- Ask: *Why does Omar imagine H_2O appearing?* (to give him courage) Describe what it means to 'swoop down'. Invite the children to describe the contrast between 'swooping down' and 'hovering'. Invite synonyms for 'hover' ('float', 'hang', 'stay close') and discuss why 'hover' is effective. (H_2O isn't on the ground – he's waiting to pounce.) Finally, ask: *What effect does H_2O have on how Omar feels and acts?* (He gives him courage to respond wittily to Daniel.)

- Provide the children, working in pairs, with copies of the Focus word table from the Scholastic website (see link on page 5). Ask them to complete the table for 'clenched', 'swooping' and 'hover'. Challenge them to choose another word from the extract to complete their sheet such as, 'unimpressed', 'towering' or 'podgy'. Provide support as they locate definitions and create sentences.

- Organise groups to re-read the extract, focusing on fluency and expression. Challenge them to use their voices to enhance the mood and drama. Can they show how Omar switches from nervous to amused to scared?

SHARED READING

Extract 3

- Read Extract 3 aloud with fluency and expression. Point out elements that informed your reading such as short sentences, exclamation marks, ellipses, commas, dashes, dialogue and text effects. Ask the children to highlight or underline these features.

- Point out how the way 'zombie' is written tells us how scared Omar and Daniel are. If you are sharing this extract after you have finished the book, revisit previous discussions on prejudice and talk about how Omar does not see the man who is trying to help them beyond how he looks and smells.

- What does 'tried to catch my breath' mean? (breathing hard and fast) Ask: *How do you think Omar is standing?* (leaning over, maybe with his hands resting on his knees)

- Ask: *How did Daniel react to the man? Was it helpful in the circumstances? How does it make Omar feel? What would you say to him if you were in Omar's position?* Invite children to imagine Omar's expressions when Daniel threw himself down (he probably looked appalled), when he imagined H_2O swooping around (he closed his eyes) and when he sat down near chewing gum (he might have turned his head, or looked revolted).

- Ask: *Why does Omar feel like a liar when reassuring Daniel?* (He is also scared and doesn't know it will be OK.) *Why is 'GROWN-UPS!' in large font?* (It indicates Omar is having an idea).

- Now ask the children, in pairs, to practise a polished reading of the extract using their voices to bring out the drama.

Extract 4

- Hand out individual copies of Extract 4 to the children. Recap on the difference between fiction and non-fiction and ask the children to identify what type of text this is. Invite the children to skim the text and identify any features of a non-fiction text. (for example: heading, illustrations, facts). Ask: *What is the format of this text?* (questions and answers)

- Ask the children, in pairs, to read the text together – perhaps one child could read the questions and the other the answers. Listen to them reading and encourage the children to support each other if they become stuck or make an error.

- Ask the children to identify the audience, purpose, language and layout of the text. Discuss how these elements are linked. (The purpose is linked to the layout, and the audience is linked to the language).

- Locate key topic-specific words such as: 'Muslims', 'Ramadan', 'Allah', 'Islamic', 'Qur'an'.

- Explore challenging words from the text such as: 'crescent', 'fasting', 'revealed', 'significance'. Ask the children, in pairs, to complete a copy of the Focus word table from the online resources (see page 5) for these words. Afterwards, share the everyday explanations, dictionary definitions and sentences the children have written.

- Tell the children to practise making notes by using the information in the text to create a mind map about Islam.

- Ask the children, in pairs, to use their mind map to recall the information they have read.

- Have a class quiz as a plenary to check how many facts the children remember from this information text.

14 **Read & Respond** Planet Omar

Extract 1

Mum had to neaten Esa up before we popped over next door, because she's embarrassed to have mucky kids.

She even said to me, 'Wait. Let me hair your run through my fingers.'

ha ha ha ha ha!

Mum says things the wrong way round when she's hurrying.

'You mean *run your fingers through his hair*,' said Maryam, because she likes to correct people.

'Yes, yes, that,' said Mum and she marched us all over and took a deep breath and rang the doorbell.

We waited.

NOTHING!

We waited some more.

NOTHING!

So I reached forward and rapped on the door, really loud, a few times.

'Why did you do that?' Mum hissed like a quiet, angry snake.

'What?' I shrugged. 'Maybe the doorbell isn't working?'

'Well, it's rude,' hissed snake-Mum, and just then the door opened quietly and eerily, like in horror movies.

There stood an old lady. Quite a short one. With lots of white hair and one of those cardigans that all old ladies wear. My grandma has one.

We all said 'Hi' pretty much together, except Esa, who said,

'Assalamu'alaikum'

like he had been taught to say to our nani.

The old lady was really weird, because she just stood there without reacting. She didn't say hello. She just stared.

Extract 2

At school, it was getting harder and harder to avoid **Daniel Green.**

One lunchtime, he came over and put a handful of sand all over my food. My stomach clenched and I got a lump in my throat. I didn't want to cry in front of him, but I was really hungry, and that sandwich, from last night's leftover chicken, was really tasty and my mouth had really been looking forward to it.

I quickly imagined H_2O swooping down from the clouds to hover right behind Daniel. I made H_2O pull a totally unimpressed face and blow steam all over Daniel's head. And Daniel had no clue.

That made me laugh and through my giggles I said loudly, 'Thanks, Daniel. Now I truly have a sand-wich.'

A few people around us started laughing too. Sarah and Ellie – girls from our class – were sitting at the lunch table next to ours and they were giggling like crazy.

Daniel stood there towering over me with his podgy fists closed tight. His face was redder than his T-shirt and he was **CLENCHING HIS TEETH** together tightly.

I pictured him as a Rottweiler dog, baring his sharp teeth ready for a fight.

Extract 3

It was the scariest thing I'd ever seen. It was terrifying and hairy and it stank. It stank so bad. It was kind of like a man, because it had a head and a body and arms and legs. But it wasn't a man. And it was dirty. So dirty. My brain told me it was a …

ZOMBIEEEEE!

Daniel screamed too.

We both ran down a long road. I looked over my shoulder. The zombie was still coming, with its arm out, trying to grab us. I ran harder.

When I couldn't see him any more, I stopped and tried to catch my breath. Daniel, on the other hand, **threw himself onto the pavement** and started wailing like never before.

I wasn't well-trained in dealing with crying bullies, or zombies. I took a deep breath and imagined H_2O flying down to help us. Swooping around to keep an eye out in case the zombie turned up again.

And then I sat down next to Daniel on the pavement. Even though there was loads of gross dried-up chewing gum on it.

I told him it was going to be OK. When I said that, I felt like a liar, because I was scared too, and I didn't really know if it was going to be OK. But that's what grown-ups always say when someone is crying – so I said it.

GROWN-UPS! What would they do right now?

Extract 4

All about Ramadan

What is Ramadan?

For Muslims, Ramadan is the holiest month of the year. During Ramadan, Muslims grow closer to Allah through prayer and fasting.

When does Ramadan occur?

Ramadan begins in the 9th month of the Islamic calendar when the new or crescent moon appears. The Islamic calendar is a lunar calendar so each year Ramadan begins 11–12 days earlier than the previous year.

It takes about 33 years before Ramadan happens at the same time of year again.

What happens during Ramadan?

Muslim adults fast during daylight hours. This means they don't eat or drink anything from sunrise to sunset. In the last ten days of Ramadan, Muslims celebrate the Laylat Al Qadr or Laylat-al-Qadr (Night of Power) – the holiest night of the year. This is when the Qur'an, the Muslim holy book, was first revealed to the Prophet Mohamed.

What can you say to someone celebrating Ramadan?

You can express good wishes to a Muslim celebrating the end of Ramadan by saying, 'Eid Mubarak' which means 'Happy Eid'.

When does Ramadan end?

When the next crescent moon appears, Ramadan ends with the festival of the breaking of the fast, Eid ul-Fitr, which lasts for three days. Friends and family gather to celebrate by sharing food and giving gifts – especially to children. Common Eid gifts for children include books, new clothes, small toys and money. Children also help decorate the home with homemade arts and crafts. The crescent moon is a symbol often used in Eid decorations.

What do children do for Ramadan?

Children don't have to fast, although some parents may allow them to fast for shorter periods.
Children are also encouraged to 'fast' in other ways like not letting themselves get angry or upset with others. They also spend time learning about the history and significance of Ramadan.

GRAMMAR, PUNCTUATION & SPELLING ▶

1. Who's talking?

Objective
To practise punctuating direct speech.

What you need
Copies of *Planet Omar: Accidental Trouble Magnet*, Extract 1.

What to do

- Use the sentence, 'OK I said slowly.' to recap on direct speech. Locate the words spoken and add the missing punctuation. ('OK,' I said slowly.)

- Provide pairs with copies of Extract 1. Ask the children to read the extract together then highlight the direct speech in the text. Ask: *How could you find the spoken words?* (the inverted commas around the words) Ask the children to highlight the inverted commas in a different colour. Ask: *How can you tell who's speaking?* (We are told before or after each direct speech.)

- Invite the pairs to create three rules for how to punctuate direct speech. Display the following words for support: 'inverted commas', 'capital letter', 'comma', 'question mark'. Afterwards, share ideas and formulate three class rules together. Display the rules on the wall.

- Locate different words for 'said' ('hissed', 'shrugged') and ask volunteers to read these lines with the correct expression, using the words for 'said' to guide their reading. Organise the children into small groups to re-read the extract with the children taking on the roles of the narrator or different characters.

Differentiation
Support: Before the session, work with the children to highlight the direct speech in a different extract. Discuss the rules for punctuating speech together.

Extension: Ask the children to scan other chapters for dialogue. Ask: *Do they follow the class rules, or do you need to create further rules?*

2. Choosing 'a' or 'an'

Objective
To use the forms *'a or an'* appropriately.

What you need
Copies of *Planet Omar: Accidental Trouble Magnet*, photocopiable page 22 'Is it 'a' or 'an'?'

What to do

- Write 'a dragon' and 'the dragon' on the board. Explain that 'a' and 'the' are articles. Demonstrate the difference between '<u>a</u> dragon' (no specific dragon/one of many) and '<u>the</u> dragon' (a particular dragon, for example, Omar's dragon).

- Read Chapter 4 aloud, asking the children to spot uses of 'a' or 'the'. Each time, reiterate the different functions of the words. Read the first two pages of Chapter 5. Invite a volunteer to read out Omar's last concern ('What if the teacher is <u>an</u> alien?') Ask another volunteer to explain why 'an' is used instead of 'a'. Make a link to the initial sound of 'alien' and agree that 'a alien' is harder to read aloud than 'an alien'. Explain that 'a' and 'an' perform the same function.

- Recap on the words 'vowel' and 'consonant'. Ask the children to locate the vowel or consonant after the article in the following: 'a lady', 'an old lady', 'a rotten apple' and 'an apple'.

- Provide the children with individual copies of photocopiable page 22 'Is it 'a' or 'an'?' to fill in.

Differentiation
Support: Provide the children with example words on cards to sort before using them on the photocopiable page. Encourage them to read the sentences aloud when deciding whether they are right or not.

Extension: Ask children to explain why '<u>a</u> useful tool' and '<u>an</u> hour' are correct although they don't follow the rule. Give a clue by asking them to listen to the initial sound of the words after the underlined article.

3. Who's in the family?

Objective
To explore word families.

What you need
Copies of *Planet Omar: Accidental Trouble Magnet*.

What to do

- Display the following word family on the board and use the words to revise root words, prefixes and suffixes: 'luck', 'unlucky', 'luckily', 'lucky', 'unluckily'. Invite volunteers to underline the root word, prefix and/or suffix in each word. Ask what the root word means and then discuss how the meaning changes when adding the suffix 'y' (changes from noun to adjective), the suffix 'ily' (changes the noun into an adverb) and the prefix 'un' (changes 'lucky' to mean the opposite). Challenge the children to suggest other words that could be in the 'luck' word family, for example: 'luckier', 'luckiest' or 'unluckiest'.

- Read the bracketed text next to the picture of Mum in Chapter 1. Focus on the word 'unimpressed' and ask the children what it means in this context, before asking them to identify the root word, the suffix and the prefix. Write 'impress' on the board and build a mind map of words in the family created using prefixes and suffixes. ('impress', 'impressive', 'impressively', 'impressed', 'unimpressed', 'impression', 'unimpressively'). Discuss how all the words are related by both form and meaning.

- Ask the children, working in pairs, to create a word family mind map for 'happy' ('happily', 'happiness', 'unhappy', 'unhappily', 'happier', 'happiest', 'unhappier', 'unhappiest'), 'active' ('actively', 'activation', 'inactive', 'deactivate', 'reactive', 'activity', 'inactivity') or 'kind' ('unkind', 'kindness', 'kindly', 'unkindness', 'kinder', 'kindest', 'unkinder', 'unkindest').

Differentiation

Support: Ask the children, in pairs, to create sentences for the words: 'luck', 'lucky' and 'unlucky'.

Extension: Challenge the children to identify the part of speech for each word in the 'impress' family and then use each one in a sentence.

4. Say when it happened

Objective
To express time using conjunctions.

What you need
Copies of *Planet Omar: Accidental Trouble Magnet*, photocopiable page 23 'Before or after'.

What to do

- Remind the children that connectives are joining words or phrases that link parts of a sentence together to tell us when (time), where (place) or why (cause) something happens. They can be conjunctions, adverbs or prepositions.

- Explain that today you are focusing on expressing time using conjunctions. Write 'when', 'before', 'while', 'after', 'until' and 'then' as a list in the middle of the board. Ask pairs of children to think of a sentence for each word, for example, 'Omar changed school <u>when</u> his mother got a new job.' Bring the class together to share sentences and write an example sentence on the board for each time conjunction – writing the sentence around each word in the list.

- Hand out photocopiable page 23 'Before or after' and ask the children to complete it individually. When they have finished, ask them to compare their answers with a friend and discuss any differences.

- Ask pairs to read Chapter 21 and to identify any time connectives showing the sequence of events or time passing, for example, 'We ran and ran <u>till</u> we reached the big space'. Then bring the class together and share what they have found and discuss other ways of expressing sequence or time that appear in the chapter, for example: using adverbials such as 'about ten minutes later', 'as soon as', 'next' or 'first'.

Differentiation

Support: Ask the children to work in pairs to complete the photocopiable page.

Extension: Ask the children to search the book for conjunctions to express cause (why), using the words 'so', 'because', 'therefore'.

5. Words matter

Objective
To explore meaning of words in context.

What you need
The children's completed Focus word tables from Shared reading of Extract 2, Extract 2, dictionaries/thesauruses.

What to do

- Display Extract 2 and circle the words 'clenched', 'swooping' and 'hover'. Ask the children, working in groups, to share their completed Focus word tables from Extract 2. Ask them to take turns to respond to these prompts: *Have you ever 'clenched' anything? Have you ever seen anything 'swooping' down? What do you know that can 'hover'?* Listen to groups working. Choose interesting responses to share with the class. Ask the groups to create new sentences for the words.

- Draw a target (a series of circles inside each other) on the board. Write the word 'clenched' in the bullseye (the middle circle). Point out where 'clenching' is used later in Extract 2, discussing whether it carries the same meaning. Now invite volunteers to suggest words or phrases with similar meanings (synonyms) to 'clenched' and 'clenching'.

- After an initial discussion, provide the children with dictionaries and thesauruses and work together to create a longer list, for example: 'tightened', 'clamped', 'gripped', 'pushed together tightly', 'held'. Write these words on the target, deciding together how close or far from the bullseye each word should be based on how close its meaning is to 'clenched'.

- Display the target and challenge the children to use any new vocabulary in their written work.

Differentiation
Support: Provide the children with a set of synonyms for 'clenched'. Discuss the meaning of each before the session.

Extension: Ask the children, working in a group, to create a target board for the word 'hover'.

6. Add ly to make adverbs

Objective
To add the suffix 'ly' on to adjectives to form adverbs.

What you need
Copies of *Planet Omar: Accidental Trouble Magnet*, photocopiable page 24 'Make that an adverb!'

What to do

- Use the words 'quietly', 'really', 'quickly', 'sheepishly' and 'slowly' to recap on using 'ly' to create adverbs. Locate the root word and suffix in each and clarify that in most cases, the root word does not change when 'ly' is added.

- Ask the children to search for adverbs in the first few chapters of *Planet Omar: Accidental Trouble Magnet*. Share their findings, for example: 'exactly', 'especially', 'sneakily', 'usually', 'angrily', 'quickly', 'correctly', 'uncontrollably', 'definitely'. Again, locate the suffix and root word. Discuss which root words were not changed when 'ly' was added.

- Use the words 'sneakily' and 'angrily' to recap on the rule for adding 'ly' to words ending in 'y'. Together, practise adding 'ly' to 'happy', 'funny' and 'sleepy'. Use the word 'uncontrollably' to recap on the rule for adding 'ly' to words ending in 'le'. Practise adding 'ly' to 'humble', 'giggle' and 'simple'.

- Write 'dramatic' and 'dramatically' on the board and ask what suffix has been added ('ally'). Invite the children to use the words 'dramatically', 'magically' and 'basically' to formulate a rule for creating adverbs from words ending in 'ic'.

- Hand out photocopiable page 24 'Make that an adverb!' for children to complete independently.

Differentiation
Support: Provide these children with a wide range of adverbs from the story and ask them to underline the root word.

Extension: Ask pairs to locate further adverbs from *Planet Omar: Accidental Trouble Magnet*. Ask them to sort their list of adverbs into sets of words with similar spelling patterns.

Is it 'a' or 'an'?

- Write the rule for using 'a' or 'an'. Use the words 'consonant', 'vowel' and 'next word' in your rule.

  _____

  _____

- Give two examples to support your rule:

  1. a _____   1. an _____

  2. a _____   2. an _____

- Complete the sentences using the correct article **a** or **an**.

  1. Mum made _____ biryani last night.

  2. Omar is hoping for _____ exciting gift at Eid.

  3. Mum calls Omar _____ trouble magnet.

  4. H_2O is _____ imaginary dragon, always keen for _____ adventure.

  5. Omar has _____ brother and _____ sister.

- Tick (✓) the sentences that are written correctly.

  1. Omar got lost at an underground station. ☐

  2. Omar had a pair of pyjamas with an dinosaur pattern. ☐

  3. Mum hissed an angry reply like a snake. ☐

  4. We bought a whole box of sweets for an Eid feast. ☐

  5. You need an umbrella with an imaginary dragon about. ☐

Before or after

> when, before, while, after, until, then

- Choose a time conjunction to complete these sentences. Use each word only once.

    1. Omar brushes his teeth _____ he goes to bed.

    2. Mum likes to sing _____ she is cooking.

    3. First, I will do my homework, _____ I will relax.

    4. Omar asked Charlie to come over _____ school.

    5. Maryam and Omar laughed _____ their sides hurt.

    6. _____ he is older, Omar might become a scientist.

- Tick (✓) the sentences that use a time conjunction.

    1. Omar needs to get to school before the bell rings. ☐

    2. Maryam enjoyed playing soccer with Charlie after school. ☐

    3. Omar felt braver because H_2O was with him. ☐

    4. Daniel glared when Omar explained what genes are. ☐

    5. The girls started giggling behind their hands. ☐

- Omar has to write a sentence at school using a time conjunction. Is his sentence correct? Explain.

    Esa hid under the bed after his nap.

    Yes/No because _____

    _____

Make that an adverb!

- Turn these adjectives into adverbs by adding the suffix 'ly'.
  Write a sentence for each adverb.

careful___	shy___	slow___	cross___	mean___

1. _____

2. _____

3. _____

4. _____

5. _____

- Look carefully at the adjectives below and what happens when you add the suffix **ly**. Write a spelling rule for each group.

angr**y** → angr**i**ly

snapp**y** → snapp**i**ly

clums**y** → clums**i**ly

How to add **ly** to adjectives ending in **y**.

_____

_____

humb**le** → humbly

simp**le** → simply

nob**le** → nobly

How to add **ly** to adjectives ending in **le**.

_____

_____

bas**ic** → basic**ally**

trag**ic** → tragic**ally**

com**ic** → comic**ally**

How to add **ly** to adjectives ending in **ic**.

_____

_____

PLOT, CHARACTER AND SETTING ▶

1. Tell it my way

> **Objective**
> To identify conventions in writing.
>
> **What you need**
> Copies of *Planet Omar: Accidental Trouble Magnet*, a range of suitable fiction titles, Extract 1 (for Support activity).

What to do

- Revise the difference between first- and third-person narrative. Invite a volunteer to tell the class what he or she did on arriving at school. Ask another volunteer to describe what their classmate did. Recap on the pronouns used in the anecdotes: 'I', 'my' and 'me' or 'he', 'she', 'his' and 'her'.
- Ask pairs to share their current reading books. Ask: *Are they story books? If so, are they written in the first or third person? How do you know?* Provide groups with a range of fiction titles and ask them to sort the books into two piles: first-person or third-person narrator.
- Now ask: *Who is the narrator in* Planet Omar: Accidental Trouble Magnet? *How do you know?* (Omar; uses 'I', 'my', 'our'; it's from his point of view) Now ask: *What is good about a character telling the story compared to an outside narrator?* (The character is in every scene; we get to know their thoughts, personal experiences, feelings and opinions about people and events.) Invite pairs to skim over the story to find examples to read out that demonstrate these features. Survey the class to find out if they enjoy this storytelling style.

Differentiation

Support: Provide the children with a copy of Extract 1 and ask them to circle the words that show that Omar is telling the story.

Extension: Ask the children to choose a chapter or scene from *Planet Omar: Accidental Trouble Magnet* and rewrite it from another character's point of view, but still in the first person, for example, the second half of Chapter 7 from the point of view of Mrs Rogers, or Chapter 19 from the point of view of Daniel.

2. Love that style

> **Objective**
> To identify how language, structure and presentation contribute to meaning.
>
> **What you need**
> Copies of *Planet Omar: Accidental Trouble Magnet*.

What to do

- Read Chapter 12 with the children, modelling fluency and expression, especially when interpreting the text effects and illustrations. Invite volunteers to read 'AMBULANCE SIREN' and 'The ambulance lights were flashing so brightly the whole room was lit up.' in a way that captures how they are written. Ask different volunteers to try different techniques, including using their voice, facial expressions and hands. Ask: *How is this more effective than just saying 'a loud, flashing ambulance siren'?* (It creates drama – as if Omar is acting it out.)
- Invite children to imitate Maryam saying, 'She doesn't deserve it,' encouraging them to explain which text features tell them *how* she says it (the size and underlining).
- At the chapter end, ask: *Who is Mrs Rogers speaking to on the phone?* (John, who might be her son, or another person she is close to, but doesn't live with) *How do you know?* (from the illustration) *How would we read this aloud?* Try different dramatic techniques.
- Now organise the class into groups and tell each group to choose another chapter to read with expression based on the illustrative text, for example: Chapter 5, 8, 13 or 16. Encourage the groups to choose different chapters. After they have practised reading together, ask them to share their chapter with another group, reading with drama and expression then explaining how the writing style added to their enjoyment of the text – if they felt it did.

Differentiation

Support: Work with groups to discuss how to interpret the text effects in their chosen chapter.

Extension: Ask the children to write a new scene for the story using a similar, graphic style.

3. All about Omar

Objective
To identify main ideas about a character.

What you need
Copies of *Planet Omar: Accidental Trouble Magnet*, photocopiable page 29 'All about Omar'.

What to do
- Organise the children into groups and hand out photocopiable page 29 'All about Omar'. Point out that some of the boxes (such as 'Omar's family') will be straightforward to fill in. Others (such as 'What makes Omar happy') will require thought and discussion.

- Tell the children, in their groups, to re-read Chapters 1 to 4 to gather evidence. Ask: *How does the author reveal Omar's character without actually describing him?* (through what he thinks, does, says, his doodles and how he reacts to situations and people) Demonstrate how to find out information backed by evidence by asking questions, for example: *How does Omar get on with his family? What tells you this? How does Omar feel about starting a new school? How do you know? Does Omar enjoy Science Sundays? How can you tell?* Model how to identify evidence in the text, drawings and dialogue to add to their Omar profiles, for example, 'We know Omar is scared of school because he gets a lump in his throat.'

- After the children have discussed each part of the profile in their group, ask them to fill in individual copies of the photocopiable page. Tell them to use key words rather than full sentences.

Differentiation
Support: Scribe for a group of children as they find evidence and answers in the text.

Extension: Ask the children to use their profiles to write a paragraph about Omar, comparing him to themselves and saying whether they would enjoy being his friend and why.

4. Being Muslim

Objective
To investigate plot, characters and settings

What you need
Copies of *Planet Omar: Accidental Trouble Magnet*.

Cross-curricular links
PSHE, RE

What to do
- Carry out this activity after reading Chapter 8.

- Revise the terms 'plot', 'character' and 'setting'. Ask volunteers to summarise the characters, events and settings found in the story so far.

- Discuss how being a Muslim is very important in Omar's life – it affects how he views the world and how others view him and his family. Ask: *Is this part of the plot, the characters or the setting?* Agree that it influences all three aspects of the story.

- Ask the children, in groups, to create a mind map for the theme of Islam in the story. Ask them to write the word 'Islam' in the centre of the page then draw three circles around it, labelled 'Plot', 'Character', 'Setting'. Ask the groups to write details about the story around each circle, for example, for 'Plot', they might write 'Ramadan', 'Fasting', 'Eid', 'Esa at the mosque'; for 'Character', they might write 'Mum wears a hijab outside', 'Maryam knows 28 surahs', 'Daniel is rude about Islam', 'Omar prays when he is worried'; for 'Setting', they might write 'mosque'.

- Revisit the activity and the children's mind maps at the end of the story. Ask: *What do we need to add to the mind map? What do we need to change?*

Differentiation
Support: Ask these children to join a group where other children can scribe for them.

Extension: Ask these children to look at Omar's diagram of his mother and a witch and discuss what it tells us about the characters of Omar, Mum and Daniel.

5. Plot the story

Objective
To identify conventions in writing.

What you need
Copies of *Planet Omar: Accidental Trouble Magnet*, photocopiable page 30 'Plot the action'.

What to do
- Revise the standard story structure: Introduction, challenge, build-up, climax and conclusion. Draw a 'story mountain' on the board. Point out where the rising action builds to the climax, and the falling action leads to the story's conclusion.

- Ask: *How does* Planet Omar: Accidental Trouble Magnet *begin? Who are the main characters? Where is the story set? What are Omar's challenges? How does he deal with them? What is the main challenge or difficulty he has to face? How does he overcome the difficulty and resolve the problem? How does the story end?*

- Hand out A3 copies of the photocopiable page 30 'Plot the action' and organise the children into groups to complete the task together. Afterwards, share the choices the children made, challenging them to explain their ideas.

- Now encourage a more thoughtful review by asking groups to discuss one or more of these questions: *Was it an engaging start to the story? Did you find the ending satisfying or could you imagine a different ending? Do you think Daniel and Omar become friends? Why? What other messages or intentions did the author have beyond telling the story itself? Did you enjoy the storytelling style? Why?*

- Share ideas together and then explain that the story is the first in a series and, encouraging reasoned answers, ask: *Would you enjoy reading another story featuring Omar? Why?*

Differentiation
Support: Limit groups to just one or two of the more thoughtful questions to discuss.

Extension: Ask the children to write a book review of *Planet Omar: Accidental Trouble Magnet*.

6. Portrait of a bully

Objective
To draw inferences about a character's feelings, thoughts and motives.

What you need
Copies of *Planet Omar: Accidental Trouble Magnet*.

Cross-curricular link
PSHE

What to do
- Carry out this activity before reading Chapter 18.

- Re-read Chapters 6 and 7. Ask: *Why did Charlie warn Omar to watch out for Daniel?* (Daniel is a bully; Daniel might be mean to Omar.) *Why is Omar confused by Daniel?* (He doesn't understand sarcasm.) Ask: *Why do you think Daniel is so mean to everyone?* Accept all reasoned answers.

- Sensitively discuss the different ways that bullies can behave, such as physical threats, verbal insults, excluding people and so on. Agree that none of these behaviours is tolerated at school. Remind the children what they should do if they are being bullied or see someone else being bullied.

- Ask pairs to search the story for the times Daniel is mean. (He throws sand, he is rude about Omar's mother and so on.) Share the children's findings. Ask: *Why doesn't Omar tell anyone about Daniel?* (He doesn't want to worry anyone; he doesn't want to tell tales.) *What does he do instead?* (He summons H_2O and says duas for protection.)

- Read Chapters 18 to 20. Ask: *Why was Daniel a bully?* (He was unhappy; he felt neglected at home.) *Does that justify his behaviour?* (No, but it helps us to understand him.) Ask: *What helps Daniel to change?* Ask volunteers to explain what we can learn from Omar and Daniel finding out more about each other.

Differentiation
Support: Discuss Daniel's behaviour in small groups.

Extension: Ask the children to write a letter to Omar from Daniel saying sorry for his behaviour.

7. Themes teach us life lessons

Objective
To investigate themes in the story.

What you need
Copies of *Planet Omar: Accidental Trouble Magnet*, photocopiable page 31 'Themes'.

Cross-curricular link
PSHE

What to do

- Recap on what the 'theme' of a book is (an idea that runs through a book). Discuss themes that the children have encountered in other books they have read, for example: courage, growing up, friendship, bullying, family, moving. Ask: *Are any of these themes in* Planet Omar: Accidental Trouble Magnet? Agree that all of them are. Ask volunteers to expand on how these themes are important to the story. Invite suggestions for other key ideas or themes in the book, for example, being Muslim, being different, respect for others, family and community, imagination, kindness, and so on. Create a long list of themes on the board.

- Hand out photocopiable page 31 'Themes' and organise the children into groups. Ask each group to choose one of the themes to investigate. If possible, organise for each group to focus on a different theme. Tell the children to look back through the story to find places where the theme is important to the plot and to think about the lesson that the author is trying to teach the reader using the theme, for example, 'Always be kind' or 'Don't judge people without getting to know them' or 'Being friends with different people enriches our life' and so on. Remind children that they might need to use their inference skills.

- Ask the children to share their completed photocopiable pages with the rest of the class. Vote on the story's most important message.

Differentiation

Support: Ask these children to focus on the theme of friendship.

Extension: Provide these children with a second copy of the photocopiable page and ask them to investigate a second theme.

8. Do I know you?

Objective
To justify inferences with evidence.

What you need
Copies of *Planet Omar: Accidental Trouble Magnet*.

Cross-curricular link
PSHE

What to do

- Ask: *How would you describe 'boys' to an alien visitor? How would you describe 'girls'?* Note their responses on the board, keeping the discussion broad and kind. Accept all appropriate answers from clothes and hairstyles to hobbies, sports and so on.

- Now ask: *Is this an accurate description of all girls and all boys?* Agree it is not and introduce the word 'stereotypes'. Explain its meaning: a very general view about someone based on one particular idea. Explain that seeing someone as a 'stereotype' can be hurtful or negative.

- Ask the children, in pairs, to divide a piece of paper in half and write the heading 'stereotype' as a heading on the left-hand side. Ask the pairs to search Chapters 2, 7, 8 and 9 for examples of Mrs Rogers' unfriendly behaviour and list these under the heading. Tell them to write at the bottom the answer to the question: *Why is Mrs Rogers rude to Omar's family?*

- Tell the pairs to write the heading 'understanding' on the right-hand side. Tell them to look for and note down examples from Chapters 12, 13 and 15 where Mrs Rogers is friends with Omar's family. Ask them to write the answer to the following question at the bottom of the column: *Why has Mrs Rogers changed?* (Omar's family helped her in a crisis; she got to know more about them and their customs.)

- Together, discuss the lesson we can learn from Mrs Rogers.

Differentiation

Support: Talk about the classic 'hero' stereotype, then compare that to real heroes who can be anyone, like doctors, people caring for the elderly and so on.

Extension: Ask these children, in pairs, to compare Mrs Rogers and Daniel.

All about Omar

- Use key words and page references from the story to build a profile of Omar.

- Draw a picture of him in the middle.

Omar's family	Omar's friends	Omar's religion
What makes Omar worried		What makes Omar happy
How Omar is brave		What helps Omar to be brave
Other interesting things about Omar		

Plot the action

- Fill in the boxes and then plot the chapters and main events of the story on the mountain.

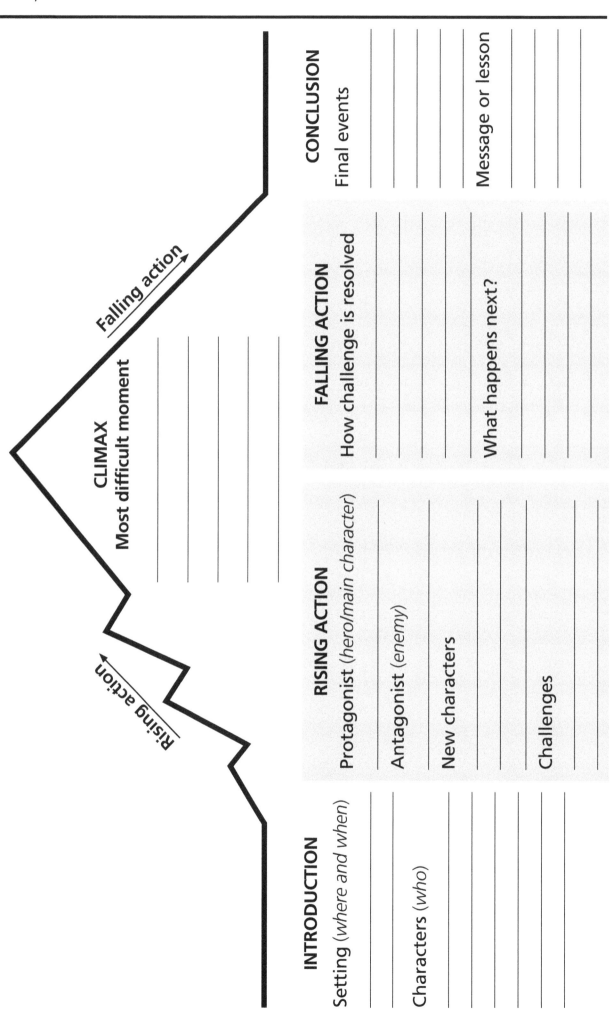

Rising action

Falling action

CLIMAX
Most difficult moment

INTRODUCTION
Setting (*where and when*)

Characters (*who*)

RISING ACTION
Protagonist (*hero/main character*)

Antagonist (*enemy*)

New characters

Challenges

FALLING ACTION
How challenge is resolved

What happens next?

CONCLUSION
Final events

Message or lesson

Themes

- Choose a theme from *Planet Omar: Accidental Trouble Magnet* and explore how it teaches the reader a lesson.

Our theme: _____

Event 1:

How does this link to the theme?

Event 2:

How does this link to the theme?

Event 3:

How does this link to the theme?

What is the author's message?

_____

_____

What can we learn from the story?

_____

_____

TALK ABOUT IT ▶

1. Q&A

Objective
To ask relevant questions.

What you need
Copies of *Planet Omar: Accidental Trouble Magnet*, photocopiable page 35 'Author interview', page 8 'About the author'.

What to do
- Together, read the author information at the back of the book then ask: *What have you learned about Zanib Mian? What else would you like to know?* Invite questions from the children, for example, 'What inspired you to write the story?' 'Who is your favourite character?' 'Have you written any other books?'

- Read aloud 'About the author' on page 8 of this book. Invite the children to listen carefully then recall the information. Together, collate the information the children can remember from both texts on a mind map on the board.

- Organise the children into discussion groups and provide each group with photocopiable page 35 'Author interview'.

- Ask a volunteer in each discussion group to take on the role of Zanib Mian. Tell the other children to take turns to ask 'Zanib' two questions – one question from the sheet and one question of their own. The child in the role of Zanib should answer the questions as well as possible.

- Afterwards, share the answers the different 'Zanibs' gave to the questions. Share the new questions the children asked and discuss which ones they were able to answer. Discuss how you could find out the answers. (look on the internet, write to Zanib Mian)

- Ask children to complete photocopiable page 35.

Differentiation
Support: Discuss possible questions and answers with these children before the role play.

Extension: Ask the children to complete the photocopiable page for another author.

2. Being different

Objective
Maintain attention and participate actively in collaborative conversations.

What you need
Copies of *Planet Omar: Accidental Trouble Magnet*, photocopiable page 36 'Differences'.

Cross-curricular links
PSHE, maths

What to do
- Read the dedication in the front of the book. Ask: *What does it tell you about the author and the story?* Share thoughts.

- Sensitively ask: *What does it mean to 'be different'? Is anyone ever exactly the same as anyone else? How would it be if everyone in the class was exactly the same? Is being different a negative or positive thing? In the story, in what way is Omar different?* Encourage the children to articulate their thoughts.

- Ask: *What makes the children in this class the same?* (their age, the school they go to, where they live, their basic needs) Ask: *What makes us different?* (our hobbies and interests, family customs, sports teams and so on) Sensitively list all appropriate answers on the board.

- Provide the children working in groups with copies of photocopiable page 36 'Differences' and ask them to use it to find out how they, as a group, are similar or dissimilar. Clarify that everyone in the group needs to participate if you are going to be able to complete the task.

- Ask: *How will you find out which four activities are most common?* (through discussion)

- Ask the groups to choose a spokesperson to share their group's conclusions with the class.

Differentiation
Support: Ensure these children are working in a group with more confident children who can help them to answer the questions.

3. What if?

Objective
To use spoken language to develop understanding through imagining and exploring ideas.

What you need
Copies of *Planet Omar: Accidental Trouble Magnet.*

Cross-curricular link
PSHE

What to do

- Write the words 'What if…' on the board. Ask: *Have you ever asked 'What if' questions? Why? Was it to imagine something positive or negative? Was it to imagine something you wished for or worried about? Can you think of a 'What if' question right now?* Share suggestions such as 'What if it snowed tomorrow?' 'What if I don't like the school lunch?'

- Read aloud Chapter 5 modelling fluency and expression. Ask: *What day is it? How is Omar feeling? Why is Omar feeling this way? What expressive ways does he use to describe the feeling in his stomach? Have you ever felt this way? What makes you feel scared or nervous?* Invite responses.

- Look at the reasons Omar gives for feeling nervous. Ask: *What do these 'what if' questions say about his state of mind? Are all the questions sensible or are some of them a bit exaggerated? Is it normal to exaggerate what might happen when you feel worried?*

- In groups, children discuss, imagine and list other 'What if' questions for someone starting a new school like Omar. Encourage them to use their imaginations to consider likely and unlikely scenarios (What if I get lost going to the bathroom? What if I have to stand in front of the class and introduce myself? What if my pen leaks everywhere?).

- Groups choose a spokesperson to read their questions to the class.

Differentiation
Support: Together, write five 'What if' questions on the board.

Extension: Ask these children to speculate on how Daniel felt before the school trip.

4. Celebrate customs

Objective
To take part in collaborative conversations.

What you need
Copies of *Planet Omar: Accidental Trouble Magnet.*

Cross-curricular link
PSHE, RE

What to do

- Write the word 'custom' on the board. Begin by explaining that the word 'custom' is a noun used to describe a certain behaviour or way of doing something by a group of people. Challenge the children to remember some customs from Omar's family, for example: Omar's family usually get up early to pray. Omar's family do a science experiment every Sunday. Omar's mother wears a hijab when she leaves the house. Ask pairs to remember further customs of Omar's family.

- Write the following topics on the board: School, Birthdays, Festivals, Weekends (adapting if appropriate, or only focusing on events at school). Ask the children, in pairs, to choose one of the topics and discuss what customs they know about. Remind them to talk collaboratively when discussing traditions that are similar and to listen with interest (looking at their partner and asking questions) when the traditions are different. Clarify that a celebration could be Eid, Christmas, Diwali, Hanukkah or any other festival they would like to choose, such as Halloween.

- Ask the pairs to feed back to the class about their chosen topic.

- If you wish to develop the topic, ask the children to share a photograph of a special custom being observed in their family. Ask them to describe the photograph and explain who is in the picture and what each person is doing.

Differentiation
Support: Use your knowledge of the children to choose a topic that they will find interesting to talk about.

Extension: Ask these children to investigate their topic further by researching customs from around the world associated with it.

5. To tell or not to tell

> **Objective**
> To participate in discussions and role play.
>
> **What you need**
> Copies of *Planet Omar: Accidental Trouble Magnet*, photocopiable page 37 'Advice for Omar'.
>
> **Cross-curricular links**
> PSHE

What to do

- Use this activity to follow on from 'Portrait of a bully' on page 27.

- Re-read Chapter 10 and the first page of Chapter 11 expressively together. Ask: *Why doesn't Omar want to tell his parents? Why doesn't he tell Maryam? Why does he decide to talk to Reza?* Invite responses backed up by reasons. Ask: *If you were in a similar situation, who would you tell?*

- Ask: *What advice would you give Omar?* Ask the children, working in pairs, to fill in photocopiable page 37 'Advice for Omar', adding three events. (being sarcastic and calling Omar names; sand throwing; insulting Omar's mother). Tell them to remember what they know about each character before suggesting what advice each character would give Omar.

- Organise the children into groups. Ask one volunteer in each group to take on the role of Omar. The other children should choose different characters from the photocopiable page. Tell the children to stand in a circle with 'Omar' in the centre. Ask the children to take turns to give 'Omar' their advice. Allow time for 'Omar' and the other 'characters' to discuss the different advice.

- Ask the children who took on the role of Omar to share what advice they received and which they liked the best.

> **Differentiation**
> **Support:** Ask children who do not want to participate in the role play to watch and offer tips and advice.
>
> **Extension:** Challenge these children to create a more detailed scene at Omar's home. Will Mum, Dad and Maryam agree on what Omar should do?

6. Find your way

> **Objective**
> To give well-structured explanations.
>
> **What you need**
> Copies of *Planet Omar: Accidental Trouble Magnet*.
>
> **Cross-curricular links**
> Geography

What to do

- Ask volunteers to explain how they get to and from school, giving detailed explanations and mentioning landmarks. Provide sentence stems such as: 'When I leave home', 'I catch a', 'We drive past', 'We walk down' and so on.

- Read aloud Chapters 18 and 19 modelling fluency and expression. Ask: *Where were the children going? How did Omar and Daniel get lost? Why didn't they know their way around? What did they do? What would you have done? What should they have done?*

- Challenge pairs to use Chapters 18 to 21 to find details of Omar and Daniel's route to the London Central Mosque. Ask them first to note down all references to the route, then take turns to describe the route to each other using sentence stems such as: 'They got on an underground train', 'They got off at', 'They crossed', 'They walked down a busy street with' and so on.

- Display an enlarged map of the area between Marylebone Station and the London Central Mosque. Circle the key landmarks from the story and ask volunteers to take turns to follow Omar and Daniel's route with their finger, describing where they went.

> **Differentiation**
> **Support:** Provide the children with cards naming the key places along the route. Ask the children to use the cards to describe where Omar and Daniel went.
>
> **Extension:** Provide the children with a London tube map. Challenge them to describe the route the boys should have taken to get to South Kensington.

Author interview

- Find out the answers to three questions below for Zanib Mian.

- Then add three questions of your own and try to find out the answers to these too.

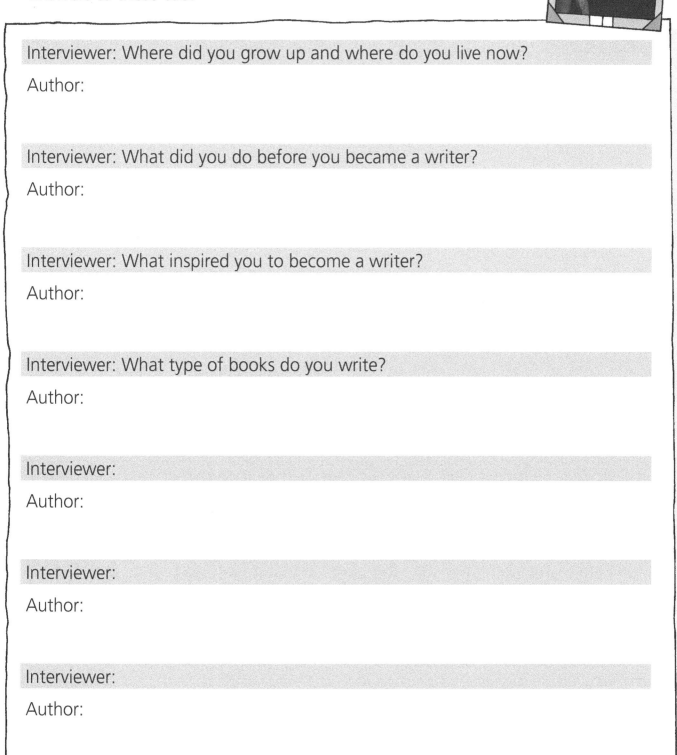

Interviewer: Where did you grow up and where do you live now?

Author:

Interviewer: What did you do before you became a writer?

Author:

Interviewer: What inspired you to become a writer?

Author:

Interviewer: What type of books do you write?

Author:

Interviewer:

Author:

Interviewer:

Author:

Interviewer:

Author:

Differences

- Work in a group to complete this survey.

1. Ask each person in your group to tick (✓) all the statements that are true for them below.

Favourite colour is blue	Prefer dogs to cats	Enjoy watching films	Like green salad	Don't like ice cream	Allergic to peanuts	Good at swimming

2. What daily after-school activities are the most common in your group? Write the four most common activities below, for example, reading, playing football, gaming, watching TV.

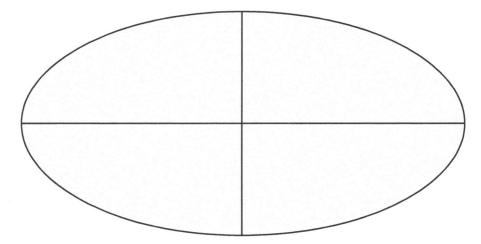

3. Complete these sentences about your group:

We are similar because: _____

_____

_____

We are different because: _____

_____

_____

Advice for Omar

- Complete the table, adding three more mean things that Daniel does to Omar. What advice would you give Omar each time?

What Daniel does to Omar	How Omar reacts	My advice for Omar

- Imagine that Omar tells someone about Daniel. What advice do you think each of these characters would give him?

Maryam	Mrs Hutchinson	H_2O
Mum	**Dad**	**Reza**

GET WRITING ▶

1. Meet the family

> **Objective**
> To discuss writing that is similar to that which they are planning.
>
> **What you need**
> Copies of *Planet Omar: Accidental Trouble Magnet*.

What to do

- Carry out this activity after reading Chapter 7.

- Together, read the character profiles at the beginning of the book. Ask: *What do you learn about each character from these profiles? Why did the author include the profiles? Do you like the style – the way it's written? Why? What do the profiles tell you about the family? Are they like your family?*

- Read Chapters 6 and 7 aloud modelling fluency and expression. Ask the children to recall the characters mentioned in the chapters and list them on the board (H_2O, Mrs Hutchinson, Charlie, Daniel, Mrs Rogers).

- Arrange the children into pairs and tell them to choose one or two of the characters from the list. Using a similar style to the profiles in the book, ask the children to write profiles for their chosen characters using information from the story so far.

- Ask the children to display their character profiles for the class to view and discuss how effective their descriptions are. Revisit the profiles after you have finished the book. Ask: *Which character profiles need to change?*

- Let the children revise or add to their profiles using information from the whole of the story.

> **Differentiation**
> **Support:** Ask the children to work with a partner to create a profile of H_2O. Provide the children with key words and phrases to use.
>
> **Extension:** Challenge these children to create characters profiles for the beginning of their own story.

2. Science Sundays

> **Objective**
> To use organisational features to plan and write instructions.
>
> **What you need**
> Copies of *Planet Omar: Accidental Trouble Magnet,* photocopiable page 41 'Science in action'.
>
> **Cross-curricular link**
> Science

What to do

- Re-read Chapter 4. Ask: *What are Science Sundays? What experiments are mentioned?* (making slime, fizzy eruptions, tornadoes in bottles)

- Hand out photocopiable page 41 'Science in action'. Ask the children, working in groups, to cut out the text and headings and stick them in the correct order onto a new piece of paper.

- Afterwards, compare the instructions the children have created. Ask: *Why is it important that the instructions are clear? Is each group's the same? What features helped you to organise the text?* Note the organisational features on the board such as main heading, subheadings, numbered steps and command verbs.

- Ask the children, working in pairs, to use the information in Chapter 4 to find out how to make a tornado in a bottle. After an initial discussion, watch a video of the experiment on the internet.

- Ask the children to write a first draft set of instructions for creating a tornado in a bottle. Provide the children with the equipment needed and ask them to use their instructions to carry out the experiment.

- Ask the children to write a final set of instructions, revising their draft if necessary and checking that they have used the features listed on the board.

> **Differentiation**
> **Support:** Ask the children to video a set of verbal instructions, using real or imaginary props.
>
> **Extension:** Ask the children to add labelled diagrams for each part of their instructions.

3. Welcome

Objective
To discuss and record ideas.

What you need
Copies of *Planet Omar: Accidental Trouble Magnet*, photocopiable page 42 'Welcome guidelines'.

Cross-curricular link
PSHE

What to do

- Begin by asking if anyone has ever moved house or school. Ask: *How did it feel? Was it easy or difficult? Did someone make you feel welcome? How did they do this? Have you ever been the person to make 'the new someone' feel welcome? What did you do?* Invite responses.

- Refer to the parts in Chapters 7 to 9 where Mrs Rogers, Omar's neighbour, reacts to the new family. Ask: *How does she behave? What could she have done differently to make them feel welcome? What things would you have done to make Omar's family feel welcome?*

- Consider Omar's first day of school. Encourage the children to refer to Chapters 6 and 7 and compare how Mrs Hutchinson, Charlie and Daniel behaved towards Omar when he arrived. Ask: *What did they say and do to make him feel welcome or unwelcome?*

- Organise the children in pairs and hand out photocopiable sheet 42 'Welcome guidelines'. Ask them to discuss each box before filling it in together. Discuss the information that will be in each box. Ask: *What warnings might you give?* (perhaps about the Wednesday fire alarm) *What tips could you give?* (Join football club on Thursdays.)

- Ask the pairs to share their ideas with the class.

Differentiation
Support: Provide the children with a simplified photocopiable page by removing the bottom section. Discuss ideas with the children before they fill in the sheet.

Extension: Write a welcome letter to Omar from Charlie with tips on what to expect at his new school.

4. Imaginary friends

Objective
To read aloud their own writing.

What you need
Copies of *Planet Omar: Accidental Trouble Magnet.*

What to do

- Ask the children to work with a partner to find the passages about H_2O in the story (Chapter 6, 10, 14, 22) and read them aloud together with expression and fluency. Afterwards, ask: *What is H_2O like? What can he do? How does he help Omar?*

- Ask: *Why does Omar have an imaginary dragon as a friend? Do you think it is a good idea to have an imaginary friend?* Encourage the children to expand their thinking.

- Ask the children to work in a group to come up with an idea for a new scene from the story where H_2O helps Omar get through a new tricky situation. It could be a lesson at school that he finds boring, a problem with Daniel, a sports lesson or a situation at home where Omar is in trouble for something he did. Ask the children to discuss their different ideas in detail then share them with the class.

- Ask the children, in pairs, to choose one of the scenarios and plan out a beginning, middle and end for the scene. The scene could be one or two paragraphs long or a whole chapter.

- Once the planning is done, encourage the children to work on their own to write the new scene.

- Afterwards, ask the children to take turns to read their scene to the class, with fluency and expression, bringing out any humour confidently.

Differentiation
Support: Ask the children to draw their new scene as a storyboard with captions.

Extension: Expect the children to create a polished scene with an imaginative use of text features and illustrations.

5. Lost and found

Objective

To proofread for errors.

What you need

Copies of *Planet Omar: Accidental Trouble Magnet.*

Cross-curricular link

PSHE

What to do

- Ask a volunteer to recap on the events when Omar and Daniel get lost. Ask the children, in pairs, to search through Chapters 18, 19, 20 and 21 to find phrases that tell us how Omar and Daniel felt when they were lost. Share the findings, for example, 'I finally managed to squeak', 'wailing like a baby', 'weed himself', 'thinking wasn't very straight', 'took Daniel's hand', 'pleaded', 'like a big lump of play dough', 'made me scream like a hyena who was about to be eaten', 'terrifying', 'ran', 'wailing like never before', 'waiting with big hopeful eyes', 'his shoulders drooped again', 'I felt a little lump in my throat', 'smiled a snotty smile', 'sounded really hysterical', 'waved at the homeless man sheepishly'. Ask volunteers to explain the emotion (upset, worry, shock, bravery, terror) captured by each phrase.

- Tell the children to rewrite the episode from Daniel's point of view. Challenge them to show (not tell) how Omar and Daniel feel. Ask: *Will Daniel be honest about crying and wetting himself? How will he describe Omar?* Remind the children to use the first person.

- Afterwards, ask the children to proofread their story, checking for spelling, grammar, errors in the story, missing words and so on. Tell the partners to first proofread their own story, and then proofread their partner's.

- Invite volunteers to share their story with the class.

Differentiation

Support: Ask the children to write a dramatic opening paragraph then spend time proofreading.

Extension: Challenge these children to read their story aloud to themselves to check for quality. Can they add adverbial phrases to improve flow? Can they add a simile or two?

6. Trouble magnet

Objective

To assess the effectiveness of their own and others' writing.

What you need

Copies of *Planet Omar: Accidental Trouble Magnet*, photocopiable page 43 'Triple trouble'.

What to do

- Ask: *Is 'accidental trouble magnet' a good name for Omar?* Unpick the importance of the words 'accidental' and 'magnet'.

- Ask the children, in pairs, to sort out the 'troubles' on photocopiable page 43 'Triple trouble'. Remember each incident, or re-read Chapters 1, 3 and 10. Discuss how each incident has a beginning, a middle and an end. Agree that the cards as they stand do not tell a funny story; challenge the children to retell each incident with a partner, adding details, bringing out the humour and using joining phrases such as 'At first', 'It started when', 'Unfortunately', 'Finally'.

- Tell the children, in their pairs, to make up their own funny anecdote about accidently getting into 'light-hearted' trouble – something true, exaggerated or completely made up. The pairs can work together on one anecdote or support each other in different anecdotes. Ask them to tell their anecdote a couple of times out loud before writing it down in a humorous manner – adding illustrations or creative fonts if possible.

- Ask the children to exchange their story with a new partner. Ask the children to say what they like about the new partner's anecdote before kindly giving advice on how to bring out the humour. Tell the children that they don't need to act on the advice they receive, but they do need to think about it and make their own judgement about the effectiveness of the humour in their writing.

Differentiation

Support: Ask the children to create a cartoon strip of their anecdote.

Extension: In groups, ask the children to create polished performances of their anecdotes.

Science in action

- This fun science activity is jumbled up. Cut out the sections and headings and reorganise them so they make sense. Paste them on to a separate sheet of paper.

4. Roll clumps of mixture into small balls and put them on waxed paper to dry.
5. Leave for 24–48 hours to dry out.
6. Store the bath balls in a dry, sealed container.
7. Add 1 or 2 to a bath and watch as they fizz away.

- 1 cup baking soda (or bicarbonate of soda)
- $\frac{1}{2}$ cup corn starch (or Epsom salts)
- $\frac{1}{2}$ cup citric acid (or lemon salt)
- 3–5 tablespoons of vegetable oil (coconut, olive, almond)
- A few drops of essential oil or fragrance oil (optional)
- A few drops of food colouring (optional)

How to make fizzy bath balls

Tips

- Try different plastic moulds to make other shapes.
- Remember to keep them away from moisture before use.

This fun activity will take about 15 minutes to complete.

Conclusion

You need

Method

When added to water, the acid and the soda react to release gas (CO_2) in the form of bubbles.

1. Combine the dry ingredients in a bowl.
2. Mix the wet ingredients in a separate bowl then slowly add to the dry ingredients.
3. Combine well until the mixture becomes like damp sand and holds together. Add more vegetable oil if needed.

Welcome guidelines

- Discuss ways that you can make a new child feel welcome in <u>your</u> class. Write notes below.

- Make a list of Dos and Don'ts then report back to the class.

Things you can say to make them feel comfortable:	Things you can do to help them:
Names of people they should know and why:	**Tips and warnings:**

How to make someone feel welcome:

DOs	DON'Ts

Triple trouble

- Cut out these cards. Sort them into three separate series of events from *Planet Omar: Accidental Trouble Magnet*. Each series of events has three cards.

- Use the event cards to tell your own funny version of what happened.

Esa starts crying and Omar's parents wake up.	Omar takes the batteries out of the remote control.	Mum and Maryam are very embarrassed.
Esa buys a whistle at the petrol station.	Omar has a bad dream.	Omar is banned from playing video games.
Esa is very noisy at the mosque.	Dad cannot watch the television and is furious.	Omar spits on Esa.

ASSESSMENT ▶

1. Dragon interview

Objective
To speak audibly and clearly.

What you need
Copies of *Planet Omar: Accidental Trouble Magnet*, Extract 4 (for Extension activity).

What to do
- Read Chapter 6 together inviting children to jump in and demonstrate fluency and expression. Ask the children to recall and share what they have learned about Omar's imaginary dragon, H_2O. Ask the children to find noun phrases and other details from Chapter 6 and share them with the class, such as 'super awesome, magnificent, dragon', 'blue and green shimmery scales', 'long swooping tail', 'almond-shaped eyes', 'tiny nostrils', breathes steam, flies at 120mph. Tell the children to search through Chapter 14 with a partner and note down any other details about H_2O, for example: 'strong tail', lives in dragon-shaped cloud, eats dragon snacks, makes it rain when he has a shower.

- Invite the children, working with a partner, to imagine an interview with H_2O. Ask them to think of questions they would like to ask H_2O. Write some questions on the board such as 'Why are you called H_2O?' or 'Who's your best friend?' 'Are you a friendly dragon?' 'Can you tell us about a time you helped a human?' Allow time for the children to role play their interview with H_2O, taking turns to be interviewer or dragon.

- Ask the children, in pairs, to practise asking and answering ten questions for H_2O, talking clearly.

- Tell the children to present their interview to the class, speaking audibly and clearly.

Differentiation
Support: Assist those needing support by modelling some questions and answers.

Extension: Ask the children to create a dragon infographic poster, combining questions, information and graphics as in Extract 4.

2. Omar-style diary

Objective
To evaluate and edit by proposing changes to grammar and vocabulary.

What you need
Copies of *Planet Omar: Accidental Trouble Magnet,* examples of diaries – on display if possible.

What to do
- Begin by asking the children if they enjoyed the book's style. Ask: *Describe features you enjoyed. Have you read other books in a similar style?*

- Together, compare the style of this book to a diary. If possible, show examples of diaries such as *Diary of a Wimpy Kid* by Jeff Kinney. Ask: *What is similar and different?* (For example, similar: first-person narrative to express thoughts and feelings, and recount events mainly in the past, with an informal, relaxed and personal style. Different: the diary format includes entries on certain days that may be addressed to a secret friend or 'Dear Diary'.) List diary-writing features on the board.

- Tell the children that they are going to be writing a diary for one of the characters in the book (except Omar), for example: Daniel, Mrs Hutchinson, Charlie or Mrs Rogers. Ask them to discuss ideas with a partner.

- Tell the children to work on their own to write a diary entry for their chosen character for one of the events in the story, using the diary-writing features as listed on the board.

- Ask the children to swap their diary entries with a partner to read and review each other's work. Tell them to suggest changes where necessary to improve consistent use of pronouns and tenses.

Differentiation
Support: Guide the children to recall first-person pronouns used in diary writing. Assist the editing process.

Extension: Tell the children to write a second diary entry using another event.

3. Omar's glossary

Objective

To use dictionaries to check the meaning of words they have read.

What you need

Copies of *Planet Omar: Accidental Trouble Magnet*, example glossaries and dictionaries.

What to do

- Display the example glossaries. Hand out dictionaries and compare the dictionary definitions to the definitions given in the example glossaries. Ask: *Is a glossary the same as a dictionary?* Agree that glossary entries are shorter and focus on how the words are used in the book.

- Explain to the children that they are going to be writing a glossary for *Planet Omar: Accidental Trouble Magnet*, for readers who are unfamiliar with Islam. Ask pairs to scan Chapter 3 and locate key words for their glossary, such as 'mosque', 'Dhuhr' 'imam', 'Rukhu', 'Sujood', 'abaya'. Locate definitions for the words in the story, supplementing definitions using a dictionary. Ask: *How is the way they are explained in the story different from a dictionary or glossary explanation?* (The definitions are informal, integrated into story, and have no references to other examples.)

- Tell the children to skim through the rest of the story and choose words for their glossary, selecting words that might not be known by all readers. Ask them to put the words into a suitable order then write a definition for each word – using the definition in the story if useful.

- Assess the choices the children make, how they organise and how they explain the words. Assess the children's understanding of the format and purpose of a glossary.

Differentiation

Support: Ask the children to focus on creating a glossary for Chapter 3.

Extension: Ask the children to create a longer glossary, incorporating as many suitable words as possible.

4. Going on a trip

Objective

To write narratives, creating settings, characters and plot.

What you need

Copies of *Planet Omar: Accidental Trouble Magnet*.

What to do

- Ask the children to remember the trip to Manchester in Chapter 11 and the trip to London in Chapter 18. Write the words 'who', 'where', 'what', 'why' and 'how' on the board and ask the children to remember each journey, answering the questions in pairs.

- Ask the children to work in groups. Tell them to take turns to tell the group about a trip they took with their family, friends or the school. Tell them to say *who* was on the trip, *where* they were going, *why* they were going, *how* they got there and *what* they did on the trip.

- Tell the children to plan a story about a trip, a holiday or a school outing where something unexpected happens. Explain that this can be based on a real event (for example, the one they told the group), completely made up or a combination of the two. Tell them to use the question words above to write notes in a mind map. Invite them to think of an exciting introduction and an interesting ending. Can they make the characters engaging? Can they describe the setting?

- Tell the children to write a first draft then swap with a partner to check and edit their story, giving advice on sense and flow. Ask them to write a final draft then read it aloud in groups, demonstrating fluency and expression.

Differentiation

Support: Ask the children to draw and label a picture with a caption or create a comic strip.

Extension: Challenge the children to extend their story and write it in the same style as the book.

5. Festivals and celebrations

Objective

To use spoken language to develop understanding.

What you need

Copies of *Planet Omar: Accidental Trouble Magnet*, Extract 4.

Cross-curricular links

RE, PSHE

What to do

- Recap on the difference between non-fiction and fiction. Ask: *Is this book fiction or non-fiction? How do you know? Can a fiction book include facts?* Agree that it can. *What facts are included in the story?* (information about Muslim traditions) Ask: *Do you think a story is a good way to learn about something? Why? Why not?*

- Write the word 'Eid' on the board. Together, create a long list of questions someone who does not know about Eid might ask, such as, 'When does it take place?', 'Who celebrates it?', 'Why is it celebrated?', 'What foods are eaten?' and so on. To support this discussion, display Extract 4 and read it together if the children have not read it before.

- Tell the children, in pairs, that they are going to be discussing a celebration of their choice using a question-and-answer format. Once they have chosen their celebration, ask them to draw up a list of questions someone might ask about it – using the ones above, or questions based on the ones in Extract 4 if they are relevant. Tell the children to discuss the answers to their questions.

- Ask the children to work on their own to write a question-and-answer non-fiction text about their celebration using their five favourite questions.

Differentiation

Support: Ask the children to focus on the talk part of the activity. Support them as they draw up the list of questions and try to formulate answers.

Extension: Challenge the children to ask questions about the festival that they don't know the answer to. Organise them to find out the answers.

6. Check your understanding

Objective

To understand what they read.

What you need

Copies of *Planet Omar: Accidental Trouble Magnet*, photocopiable page 47 'Reading for meaning'.

What to do

- Read Chapter 10 aloud to the children. Display the following questions on the board: What did Daniel say to Omar that made him feel very anxious? Why did it upset Omar? Why didn't Omar talk to his parents? Why didn't he talk to Maryam? Ask the children to discuss each question in turn with a partner then write their answer in their book. Discuss the answers the children have written. Ask: *Which questions could you answer by finding the answer in the story? Which questions needed you to use your inference skills?*

- Prepare the children for the comprehension activity. Revise general comprehension techniques: reading the questions carefully, working out if the question needs them to find the answer in the text or use their inference skills. Model skimming the text for context and clues, scanning for details and specific information, checking the meaning of unfamiliar words in context and so on.

- Ask the children to re-read Chapter 11 then answer the questions on photocopiable page 47 'Reading for meaning', writing full answers in their books or another piece of paper. Remind the children to refer to *Planet Omar: Accidental Trouble Magnet*.

- Assess the children's ability to answer the questions independently, demonstrating their comprehension skills.

Differentiation

Support: Limit the number of questions children answer. If appropriate, scribe for the children so they can focus on finding or inferring the answers.

Extension: Ask the children to write five questions of their own for a partner to answer. Challenge them to include both retrieval as well as inference questions.

 # Reading for meaning

- Read Chapter 11 of *Planet Omar: Accidental Trouble Magnet* and answer the questions in detail. Write your answers on another piece of paper.

1. Which word tells you that Omar cannot wait to talk to Reza?

2. What does Omar want to ask Reza?

3. Why is Reza the person Omar decides to talk to about his problems?

4. Who is Reza and how old is he?

5. Where does Reza live?

6. Find and copy a sentence that tells you that there are many Muslims living in Manchester.

7. Give **two** reasons why Omar loves to visit Reza.

8. What does Omar think of Reza? Why?

9. Why does Dad say 'I told you so' on every trip?

10. What might Mrs Rogers be thinking as she watches Omar's family leave for their trip?

11. Why didn't Reza enjoy his trip to Pakistan?

Available in this series:

978-1407-15879-2

978-1407-14224-1

978-1407-16063-4

978-1407-16056-6

978-1407-14228-9

978-1407-16069-6

978-1407-16070-2

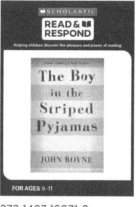

978-1407-16071-9

978-1407-14230-2

978-1407-16057-3

978-1407-16064-1

978-1407-14223-4

978-0702-30890-1

978-0702-30859-8

To find out more,
visit www.scholastic.co.uk/read-and-respond